Tales From Hampshire

Edited By Emily Wilson

First published in Great Britain in 2017 by:

Young Writers
Remus House
Coltsfoot Drive
Peterborough
PE2 9BF
Telephone: 01733 890066
Website: www.youngwriters.co.uk

FOREWORD

Young Writers is proud to present, 'Welcome to Wonderland –
Tales From Hampshire'.

For our latest competition, we invited secondary school pupils to
write a hundred word story set in a fantasy land or alternative
world of their own creation. This could be a positive magical place
where dreams come true or a dark, war-torn climate.

Dystopian fiction is hugely popular with young adult readers and
this competition gave aspiring writers the chance to create their
own vision of what the future could be like, from totalitarian
politics to post-apocalyptic landscapes. The results are
imaginative, insightful and often frightening.

Although it's a difficult task to bring a whole new world to life in
such few words, pupils rose to the challenge in creating their
Wonderlands, making use of descriptive language and building
atmosphere. The resulting collection is diverse and fascinating,
containing everything from natural disasters to futuristic lands
where technology has taken over.

I would like to congratulate all the authors featured in this
anthology and I hope it encourages you to keep writing!

Emily Wilson

CONTENTS

Rosie Farmer (13)	61
Ethan Doherty (13)	62
Jack Kemp (15)	63
Kira Thorn (15)	64
Lauren Wood (12)	65
Charlotte Quinn (13)	66
Sam Coker (12)	67
Katy Jayne Laidler (13)	68
Hollie Keeling (12)	69
Oliver Doughty (13)	70
Jack Cox (15)	71
Rosie Pearce (14)	72
Rohan Mohindra (13)	73
Josh Obeney (13)	74
Logan Thomas Bottomley	75
Emily Muncey (15)	76
Eleanor McGeachy (13)	77
Morgan Barrass (15)	78
Ben Edwards (13)	79
Maya Ray (12)	80
Jamie Clegg (13)	81
Tyler Darley (11)	82

Oaklands Catholic School & Sixth Form College, Waterlooville

Ruthie Quinn (12)	83
Bethany Kate Saunders (12)	84
Katherine Esther Gamboa-Kerwood (12)	85
Emily Poppy Lipman (13)	86
Athene Ryan (12)	87
Beau Rimmer (12)	88

The Clere School, Burghclere

Charlie Knight (13)	89
Mollie Johnson (12)	90
Lewis Samuel Williams (11)	91
Ellie-Anne Stoodley (13)	92
Jamie Harrison (12)	93
Cody Logan Marsh (13)	94
Jonny Powis (12)	95
Jack Kitson (11)	96

Libby Machin (13)	97
Angus Mills (13)	98
Miki Jarzembowski (12)	99
Amandi Mendis (12)	100
Genevieve Jacklin (12)	101
Tyler Sean Alison (12)	102
Amy Hopgood (11)	103
Danny Pither (12)	104
Kenzii Aitken-Thompson (11)	105
Lauren Ann Osborne (13)	106
Cerys Deakin (12)	107
Hannah Gaff (12)	108
Cameron Vincent (13)	109
Libby Jonas (11)	110
Jonathan David Spence (13)	111
Darcy Drummond (12)	112
Lily Soper (13)	113
Cameron Digance (13)	114
Thurka Ananth (12)	115
Phoebe Maxwell-Heron (12)	116
William Hunter (12)	117
Katie Smith (13)	118
Nathan Cook (11)	119
Emily Grace Bentham (11)	120
Aaron Cinnamon (11)	121
Zachary David Morgan (12)	122
Adam Lee Goater (13)	123
Megan Holmes (13)	124
Millie Leonard (13)	125
Madeleine Rose Gant (12)	126
Caitriona May Langrell (13)	127
Alfie Knox (13)	128
Henry Munslow-Barker (14)	129

The Island Learning Centre, Newport

Josh Logan (14)	130
Shaun Anthony Joseph Moore (15)	131

The Romsey School, Romsey

Jake Mitchener (12)	132
Haiden Crook (13)	133
Reece Grimshaw (12)	134
Rebecca Allison (15)	135
Cameron Davis (13)	136
Gareth Lewis-Cole (12)	137
Oliver Pace (13)	138
Olivia Taylor (12)	139
Reuben Burbidge (13)	140
Jessica Sedman-Lambe (14)	141
Chris Blake (13)	142
Jessica Beauchamp (12)	143
Jean-Luc Hill-Dobson (13)	144

THE MINI SAGAS

Good Or Evil?

The candles went out, the room was dark. 'Argh!' Blair
blurted out this frightful scream.
'You've never screamed like that, it's like you're a different
person,' said Emily in a trembling voice.
'Turn the lights on,' shouted Blair, pointing at the lights. The
lights flickered and came on. The girls realised it worked.
The girls started walking through the hallway at school.
The mean girl shouted sarcastically at Blair and Emily. 'The
witches, run!' The girls stood staring into her soul, were they
going to use their powers for good or evil? And get the
revenge. What did they choose?

Charlotte Linda Butler (15)
Aldworth School, Basingstoke

Syndicate Creed Age Of Greed

'There,' breathed Jacob as he threw the last rock into the Thames.

'There, there? What the hell do you mean, there? We still have reinforcements arriving to kill us you bleedin' buffoon,' screeched Evie at Jacob.

'So these are the rats that eat and steal from us,' murmured a strange voice.

Quick as a flash, Jacob and Evie whipped around to identify the stranger, only to be met with the butt of rifle and then black. Awakening from their forced slumber they heard only dripping then steps. Was it their future approaching or the cold heartless hands of their death?

Marcus Steele (14)

Aldworth School, Basingstoke

The World Beyond...

The children entered the house, wondering what was to happen next. They crept around. The children were called Jasper, Katie and Daniel and the trio had no idea about what Katie was about to discover. 'Hey guys,' called Katie, 'Why is that door glowing?'

They opened the door and stepped through the portal to find what looked like a computer room, but as Jasper looked closer they discovered 'they' were controlling their best friends! When they plucked up the courage to ask them, they explained it was a human workshop and they controlled humans and used them for everyday work!

Danielle Katie Harrington (14)
Aldworth School, Basingstoke

The Manor House Of Evil Spirits

Stranded in the eerie woods, the girl wandered with a fearful look plastered across her face. Trembling uncontrollably, she gazed into the distance; a frightening figure caught her eye. It couldn't be, a haunted house? It was a dilapidated mansion camouflaged in overgrown flora. Edging closer to the monstrosity before her, she couldn't contain her curiosity. Like a mouse she crept timidly towards the door, the deafening silence enough to make anyone flee, but the door was open ajar and she persisted on... but then her stomach churned for she realised where she was... 'The Manor House of Evil Spirits'...

Maisie Howard (13)
Aldworth School, Basingstoke

Octavius The Demon

Octavius was bored. The under-realm didn't have any beings feeble enough to destroy. It remembered the unearthly joy it felt at being released onto Planet Earth! Octavius had emerged silently into a dark, candlelit room. Pathetic creatures huddled around it. It swiftly blew open the small room and used telepathic powers to savagely rip the planet clean in two. Countries crumbled like chalk. Fire erupted to form a cage around the puny things. They screamed silently as they boiled and blistered in their rubbery skins. Octavius stared in awe; a stone statue, stuck still in a world of stomach-turning chaos.

Will Pragnell (14)
Aldworth School, Basingstoke

Prisoners

So, I was just walking along to the food area, thought Alf.
'What do you think you're doing?' said the robot.
But before Alf could reply, the robots started beating him up.
He didn't have the chance to call for help because he was
out cold after five minutes.
'Alf!' called Hank. Hank didn't know what was going on but
when he got to Alf he freaked out. 'I'll kill you!' shouted Hank
as he rushed over to destroy the robots, then everyone in
the the whole prison broke loose and back-up was called.
'I rule this prison,' said Alf.

Michael Gibbs (14)
Aldworth School, Basingstoke

The World After Life

It was dark. I didn't know where I was, all I could see was Mitch moving into my face. I whispered, 'What's happening?'

Mitch distortedly replied, 'Steve, he's gone, they took him!'

My face dropped. I started crying. 'He was my brother and I lost him,' I cried to Mitch.

He dramatically told me that they blew up the city above us. He exclaimed, 'They're going to find us, they're going to get in here. We're going to die.'

This was when I realised they had us on lockdown. It was the grey head aliens and they're coming now!

Luke Kiefer-Smith (13)
Aldworth School, Basingstoke

Untitled

The air is thick, the ground covered in remains. It is too much for me to take. I can hear groans in the background, I look over to Kyle. He looks worried, 'We should hurry up. They're getting close.' The word 'they're' sends chills down my spine. Smelling the rotten flesh and blood makes me feel sick. We're all sick really, with the amount of disease going around.
The undead catch up, causing four of us to get our guns out. I get a baseball bat out. We attack, blood goes everywhere. I can hear screams, we won't survive.
'No!'

Chloe Ann Hawkins (14)
Aldworth School, Basingstoke

Welcome To Wonderland

I looked around, it was barren, dead and lifeless. I turned around, there was this crazy-looking man standing there. He said, 'Hello Tom, how are you?'

I said, 'Fine. Where am I?'

The man looked surprised, he said, 'This is your world, you created it, you can do whatever you want without consequence. Whatever you desire.'

I was shocked, I imagined my dead dog, Lucky. I turned around and he was there. Lucky jumped on me and I asked the man again, 'Where are we?'

He said firmly, 'This is your world, your reality, your Wonderland, Tom.'

Kieran Dredge (14)
Aldworth School, Basingstoke

The Oracles Of Werville

I slowly stood and brushed the layers of dust off my robes. I was in the now destroyed town: huts, non-existent, the temple ablaze. Something broke through the clouds rapidly descending but it disappeared behind the distant mountains as quickly as it appeared. I wondered what it was. Five silhouettes emerged ominously from the gloomy neck of the valley. They were a five-man army advancing in formation. They stopped before me and dismounted. The leader approached me and declared, 'We thank ye for thy help. In return we proclaim you wizard of Werville.' And then the extraordinary adventure began.

Jack Dilly (14)
Aldworth School, Basingstoke

The Life Of Dawn Saunders

There once lived a girl called Dawn Saunders. She was secretly a witch. One morning, she was hanging out with the love of her life, Oliver Pope. Dawn was having the time of her life... Suddenly, a bright light burst forth from her delicate hands. Passers-by stared at her, angrily shouting, 'Witch!' They advanced on her with torches and pitchforks. The villagers chucked her in the river with ropes around her arms and legs. Fearfully, Oliver jumped into the freezing water, racing to get to Dawn's lifeless body, which was sinking fast. He managed to grab it, saving her life.

Elisia Hart (14)
Aldworth School, Basingstoke

Kishmar

Uneasy silence settled across the caved vault. Various cracks and howls echoed through the mountain. I backed away from the emperor, sensing he was the likely target. The double gates quaked at the distant end of the strong room. A deafening shriek followed; the Kishmar army ruptured through the gates, leaping over the heaps of treasure. I sprinted to my right, seeking the hidden trapdoor. My sight took me to Kebron, he had darted to the lever which initiated the trap sequence. The Kishmar were closing in on the emperor without hesitation. Then a black smoke consumed the vault...

Jake Pearce (14)
Aldworth School, Basingstoke

Weaker Soul

We are the rejects of Earth. The country we were from never really mattered, or the colour of our hair. Not even our personalities, ironically. In fact, I don't think even the world we came from matters, although they have tried to keep us apart. 'Tried' being the key word here. Everyone thinks we are the only person in our bodies, the only soul. They're wrong. We don't really like telling them though. You're just the most powerful one. The 'voices' we hear aren't voices, they are just the weaker souls. It's not madness, it's part of who we are.

Melinder Kaur (13)
Aldworth School, Basingstoke

Underfoot

Silence... That's what we wished for. The sound from underneath our feet was constant; a dark rumbling noise deep and ominous. The population of Earth shrank from nine billion to 100,000 in under two weeks. Those who survived the initial explosion were killed by an infection and those who survived that suffered the worst fate, being hunted down by the cryodrones, the aliens that came with the meteor. That day we attempted to take a small town, we believed it was desolate. As we walked through the gate there was a deafening silence. Then... they attacked, quietly and quickly.

Ashton Harrison Cooper (14)

Aldworth School, Basingstoke

The Aftermath

I emerge from the underground stations, fists clenched, not knowing what to expect from the land I used to know. Corpses peppered the mossy, broken streets. I look around my town, seeing my friends and family lying there lifeless. All I can think of is if I am the only one or not and where they can be.

I walk through the streets looking at the decomposing corpses, wondering how long since the explosion. As I walk through the streets going deeper into the heart of the city the atmosphere becomes eerie. Then the overgrown buildings start to shake violently...

Brandon Avenell (14)
Aldworth School, Basingstoke

Andromeda At War?

On a planet called Andromeda, a huge war broke out between two races; humans and krogans. The war was over territory and wealth. This war of rage and bloodshed lasted several months. Over these months thousands of civilians were injured or killed during the terror. The krogan battle master and shepherd (the commanders of the two races) were calling troops from different galaxies to Andromeda to help fight the war.

Eventually the war was put to peace because of the amount of casualties caused and half of the city was left in ruins. Andromeda was finally at peace.

James Cook (15)
Aldworth School, Basingstoke

Back To Front

Hannah cautiously slid across the frozen pond. She couldn't turn back now. Suddenly, a crack appeared by her torn, muddy boots. Panicking, Hannah screamed and stumbled backwards and let out a yelp whilst being rapidly consumed by the freezing darkness below. Everything seemed to flip upside down and back to front as she cannonballed into a much warmer and bluer version of the pond, she'd fallen into. As Hannah's head bobbed above the water, she realised it was summer. She saw a couple staring at her like she was a stranger. They were Hannah's parents. Who was she?

Deeya Dasgupta (13)
Aldworth School, Basingstoke

The Final Four

The final four stood. Awaiting death was torturous, the fiery mass burning around them. Stood in deafening silence, only panicked breath could be heard. Each thought entailed the same idea, the utopia they ceased to inhabit. If that wasn't enough, an escape could've existed, if only they were faster. The ruler was to blame, however he was the saviour too. He built the planet up from the ground with only his two hands, yet crushed it with them too. He was resented, but now, with the end approaching, they were ever regretful of thinking their old lives were arduous ones...

Ellie Walker (14)
Aldworth School, Basingstoke

Sanity

Daraco. A world thought to be Hell's brother. Where families were brutally divided and affection unheard of. Daraco was led by fear and darkness, until it all changed.
A young girl named Sophia was born in this world described as dystopia. Sophia was the only one who knew it wasn't perfect, she hadn't been driven insane by King Damien. Sophia never let him and his demons slither like snakes into her brain. Sophia found what she believed was happiness. When she read in-between her shifts waiting to the king. She read about a world which had love. She found it.

Yasmin Spratling (14)
Aldworth School, Basingstoke

The World Next Door

It felt like the perfect curse. Esterfay was heaven. But, I preferred Fellwyn - it was like a nightmare. It's what I was used to. Esterfay was charming, wonderful and, dare I say it, peaceful. Fellwyn only contained fighting, unrest, and hatred for others. The people of Esterfay talk to me as if we'd already met. They even know my name. As I was getting lost in my mindless, meaningless, melancholy thoughts, a loud crash brought me back out of them. Looking up from my hands, placed in my lap, I saw something I'd never dream of in Esterfay. A fight.

Gemma Blomquist (14)

Aldworth School, Basingstoke

The Story Of Moonstruck Valley

It was a cold and morbid morning, only four people survived the zombie apocalypse. Everyone was cheerless but one, he was the mayor, because he planned to change his dystopian town into something new, like no one's ever seen before! He gave his speech as proud as a lion but no one could see his vision.

Several months passed and the mayor's vision was now real, his dystopia was now his utopia, but something was wrong... He still wasn't happy, but what was it? After many weeks, he cracked and went insane with power! Who lived to see the results?

Harry Blunden-Parsons (14)
Aldworth School, Basingstoke

The Final Frontier

The sun, it seemed, illuminated the surrounding planets in its solar system, but there was one which lingered in the shadows, as if it were a demonic and vague presence haunting space itself. 'Not much longer now,' I muttered. 'As long as we stay together,' said Foster, my co-pilot. 'I hope so my friend,' I answered as I peered out into the vastness of space. I noticed a sudden flicker of light growing larger by the second. 'Could it be? Eject!' *Boom!* We were now all alone, floating in the black abyss of space...

Thomas Blissett (13)
Aldworth School, Basingstoke

Foreverland

Hundreds of years ago, a world was created known as Foreverland. It was known for its tiny people, who built quaint little treehouses that lit up in the moonlit sky. From dawn to dusk they collected water from the stream. They bathed in the crystal-clear waterfall. It was a very happy place, the plants bloomed ferociously and the flowers sang happily. Until they were invaded by tiny giants, who tried to take leadership of this beautiful world. They tore everything apart until it was bare land. The tiny tree people fled as they cried, 'We will never come back!'

Aleisha Lentell (13)
Aldworth School, Basingstoke

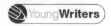

Confusion

I woke up, lost. Where was I? I only remembered going to sleep the night before... I've never seen this place. Was I even on Earth anymore? Restless, I stood up from lying on cold, hard stone ground and began to wander around this eerie universe.

After walking around for what seemed like hours, I eventually found what I thought was a human. I approached them and started talking, asking them questions. They didn't understand me. They gave me a look of blind confusion and in deafening silence, they walked off. Was I ever going to make it home alive?

Mya Bradford (14)
Aldworth School, Basingstoke

The Other Side Of The Water

It was a cold, dark night and Della was gazing out the window. Della had never wanted to move to Silvermoon Hill, she was beginning to think it was the reason for her bad luck.

One night, while Della was trying to sleep, she heard a voice call, 'I'm coming for you, Della!'

This pushed her over the edge; she ran outside in terror. She could barely see in the thick mist and as she fled from the cries, the mist surrounded her. She screamed as she plunged into the icy water. She knew her ghost would never escape again.

Alice Goveas (15)
Aldworth School, Basingstoke

The Meeting

It was a bright summer's day in 3104 when a big something covered the sun causing darkness everywhere. It was very strange-looking, almost alien-like, it had no wings, it just seemed to be hovering over everything, its shadow covered all the roads and buildings. After about an hour of it staying in the same place it started to lower slowly. Everyone was frozen with fear, the silence was deafening. Once it had fully touched the ground everyone stood back. The door opened slowly. As it opened people slowly started to see what was inside. What would happen next?

Alfie Long (13)
Aldworth School, Basingstoke

World Of New Life

Decades, me and my companions have travelled from the repulsive Planet Earth to our current location, Mars. Searching for a new life which is equal and money free. Where no one has to take leadership and we all live by our own legislation. In a society where it is crime-free. We may be dead but we are self-sufficient.

Hours I have been swaying in the wind, smiling like a kid in a candy shop and felt ecstatic that I am here, not Earth. *Bang!* Looking to my left, there I spot an aeroplane. This can only mean one thing...

Jodie Cole (15)
Aldworth School, Basingstoke

The Beast

Staring into its beaming eyes, with deep thought. *Will this be my last breath?* I pondered. The beast took a few steps towards me, his eyes still fixed upon me. With every breath I took my heart sank deeper, deeper and deeper. Its large paws continued to step until we were eye to eye. Practically touching. Its smoky breath steamed up my glasses like a burning house. The stench of its oozing nose circled around until it reached me, travelling down my throat. It began to groan louder and louder. *Is this the end?* I thought to myself, in fear.

Megan-Jayne Bartlett (15)
Aldworth School, Basingstoke

Detramus, The Slave Planet

A new planet called Detramus. The ruler owns a lot of slaves. He worships a different kind of religion. They have a new god called Detize. He has over 20 million slaves, they all worship the same religion.

He is under attack by an unknown planet. They're firing lots of lasers at Detramus. Over five million of the slaves have already been killed so they build a bunker to hide in while they are under attack.

The attack stops, everyone gets out to see if the planet is safe. As soon as they get out, a bomb strikes the planet.

Amanda Jarrett (14)
Aldworth School, Basingstoke

Untitled

It was a prodigious discovery far beyond human comprehension. With the press of a button I could change everything. A parallel world to ours, everything so perfect; no poverty, no war, no worries. Heaven? The decision of my life a button away. Yet so close but so far. Was it really perfect? Is this what the world needed, was time and money the answer. The world's population decreasing as time went by, people in urge to get away, consumed by greed without a second thought they would be gone. In a parallel dimension, far, far away from reality and humanity.

Sema Coskun (15)
Aldworth School, Basingstoke

Horseyland

Maizie is a brown horse who loves jumping and running and in her free time she likes to eat lots of grass. Maizie loves being ridden and she is a super behaved pony when she goes to a show.

One day a fairy came to visit Maizie, and the fairy saw how well-behaved and beautiful Maizie was and so she offered her a deal. She said if Maizie could run her back to her family then she would reward her with a special gift.

So Maizie ran as quick as she could and the fairy turned her into a unicorn.

Alisha Price (14)
Aldworth School, Basingstoke

Ruby Red

A smash of glass. A piercing shriek. Emmeline dropped the stack of books which originally towered in her arms. The library surrounding her was a maze, every turn led her to somewhere she didn't want to be. Emmeline would have fled if not for the booming footsteps of the intruders. Every eight o'clock the queen would read. But as soon as the girl reached her queen's favourite armchair, she let out a silent scream. Adjacent to the chair was the monarch, her blood as red as her ruby-jewelled crown; a man with a long bloodied knife stood up...

Myá Graves (14)
Aldworth School, Basingstoke

All Alone

Alone, separated from his group, the dying survivor slowly sprinted towards what seemed as his fate. The post-apocalyptic world had gotten the best of him, it got everyone. The zombies were closing in on him, like the walls were moving. The only place he could have gone is up, up into the tall trees. Half dead, he managed to scramble up the bark, and onto a large branch. His heart was slowing, it was as cold as ice. The dead, decomposing devils began climbing, trying to reach their victim. Before they approached, the poor man had already turned.

Steven Parker (14)
Aldworth School, Basingstoke

The Ghost Without Answers

It's been said by my co-workers that a ghost of a woman has been seen many times on our construction site, she's been said to wear a white flowing dress with matching headdress and similar shoes with silver locks that reached her hips tied back into a plait. They said she used to work at the site before the incident that occurred on her wedding day and she wanders through the area, searching for her husband and some answers.

They turned to look at me with horror in their eyes. I smiled at my once good friends and slowly vanished.

Amelia-Rose Bryant (15)

Aldworth School, Basingstoke

The Aliens And The Jewels

It was a cold, wet and miserable day in London. It was early morning, so everyone was just starting their day, including Joseph, a weird yet wonderful alien that was mysteriously hanging out around the Tower of London. He looked suspicious, so he must be up to something but nobody was sure what. All of a sudden a huge gust of wind swept across the whole of the Tower of London. Just then, the alarm went off so either an evacuation was happening or much worse. Everyone was stunned. Suddenly the police ran into the museum but it was unoccupied.

Ben May (14)
Aldworth School, Basingstoke

The Suspicious Island

I'm stranded on an island, it's the most repulsive and joyless place I've visited. Last night at around seven there was the most uncommon and daunting noise I've heard. I've never been so scared... Moments after I heard this noise, screams followed. I looked over in the distance then I saw a man and woman in a boat. He hit her... She was screaming to him to get off her. The boat was beginning to approach the island I'm on. It slowly touched the sides of the island, he dragged the woman off, leaving blood trails.

Gracie Smith (15)
Aldworth School, Basingstoke

Chosen

I wake up blinded by lights from screen-covered walls. A metal panel opens, arrogantly offering a vial of purple liquid. It burns my throat as always. Life was simple at home, before they brought me here, technology wasn't like this. That familiar feeling of dread creeps up my body as I see them, the men coming to take me to my daily task. Apparently the world is ending, they said they brought me here two years ago to protect me. Every day I choose one innocent person to die, because I have the power. It's about time I get answers.

Lucy Quillin (14)
Aldworth School, Basingstoke

The Town

The air is full of devastation. Smoke covers the sky like a black cape, filling my nose with a smell of burning. A boom rings in my ear like church bells. A great ball of fire blasts up in the air like it's come from the belly of a dragon! Bodies of people I know and love lie in the street, again a rumble from underground shakes the town, bringing more buildings down. I shake with fear as more explosions go off and more buildings crumple like paper. A figure appears behind me and whispers, 'It's just us two left.'

Andrew Brady (15)
Aldworth School, Basingstoke

Gateway To Freedom

'Run!' was the only thought that flashed through my mind. Every day, the urge grew greater. But how would I know if it was truly freedom? It drew me in like a cosy bed, but yet whenever I drew near I was pulled back. When I came of age, they would present me my medallion. I knew it. I'd seen it done before, to those few who had passed through, and returned beaming. The giants would often widen the gateway, although making sure I could not pass through. At last, the cat was given his collar. He rushed towards the catflap.

Benjamin Wall (13)
Aldworth School, Basingstoke

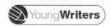
A World Of Opportunities

Only five more minutes until we start the descent. I cannot wait. It's been such a long time now, I'm kind of getting nervous. Just thinking how long I have been waiting for this day is making my legs tremble. I don't know what they will think of me, or if they will consider me being a part of their organisation. As I step off the plane I can feel their piercing eyes on me, I sort of feel embarrassed. I don't know why. I don't get it. We are all human but somehow we are very different people.

Alfie Cooper (15)
Aldworth School, Basingstoke

Alien Abduction

Bang! There was a blinding blue light that appeared suddenly, making me hide my face. I started to feel a tug on my arms, then my body. I was scared. I hesitated to open my eyes, once I did the blue light was gone. It was silent. After about ten minutes I started to hear sounds which were hard to make out. All of a sudden it went silent again, so I called out. Straight after I called out there was a screeching scream. I panicked and looked around but all there was, was darkness. I heard elephant-like footsteps...

Ryan Baker (15)
Aldworth School, Basingstoke

The Infinite McDonald's Food

Three young boys walked into McDonald's to order some food and when they finished eating they all went to the bathroom and looked at the mirror and it was saying: 'Enter me'. So they jumped straight through and they woke up and they were in a quiet and foggy place so they stood up and saw lots of trees around them. They began to walk forwards and they then found a huge table of infinite McDonald's food so they jumped on the table and stuffed their mouths with Big Macs, chips, McFlurries and more.

Joshua Lee Cotterill (14)

Aldworth School, Basingstoke

The Bunker

Fifteen years ago my life changed forever. It was the second of January when Vicar Vabao told me the world was going to end the following day. Even though he had no proof, I felt if I didn't I would be being unloyal to God and the church. I think this is how Doris got there as well, but we never talked about life before the 'world ending'. Life inside the bunker was hard, always some job that Vabao would make us do. No light entered, so we used to write about what life was like outside the bunker...

Sophie Hughes (13)
Aldworth School, Basingstoke

Now He's Gone!

I could feel it. I knew it was going to happen. I heard them banging on the door; they came flying in like a bullet from Evil's gun. They ran up the stairs, thudding like a herd of wild elephants. He silently screamed as they dragged him down the staircase; I saw it in his face. I despised how much control they had over everybody and how they made the police take my brother away from me. I turned to see the gang of hooded teens watching. I knew that he shouldn't have spoken to them. Now he is *gone!*

Erin Riggall (14)
Aldworth School, Basingstoke

Superpower World

As I approached the world of incredible superpowers, I saw a ball of fire waiting for me to take. I took the ball of fire and then had a variety of options to choose my very own superpower. There were 50 options, such as flying, speed, strength, mind-control, etc. But I was unique, and I chose to have the force! After I chose my option, I then entered the world of superpowers. I saw people flying, running and doing all kinds of magical tricks, it was brilliant. So all I had to do for now was to be a hero...

Joshua Hugh Lavery (15)
Aldworth School, Basingstoke

Ninjaland

Once, there was a girl called Nicola who lived on Mars in a place called Ninjaland. She was very lonely and had no one to play with. She prayed that there could be more people for her to play with. The next morning she woke up and there were loads of people that looked just like her. The problem was that she prayed for more people to play with but there were aliens too. She didn't like that. She met up with all her new friends and had a meeting and they worked together and got rid of all aliens!

Nina Thomas (15)
Aldworth School, Basingstoke

Fallen Utopia

The place was cold and desolate, yet a strange, ominous feeling drew up my back as if someone was watching my every move. As the cool afternoon breeze came through it rustled the dead, wounded tree as it went through the concrete jungle of which was once a utopia. I sat down, thinking of what to do next. I heard a noise, it was something that I've never heard of before and it was coming closer, every tick of the clock made me grow more and more anxious. *Tick-tock, tick-tock...* until it came.

Thomas Malone (14)
Aldworth School, Basingstoke

Taldow And The Sinking Fear

I awake to the sound of a fierce wind hitting me like a rock, the sky is all I can see as a voice says to me, 'Look forth for guidance.'
I am confused as I sit up while the sky turns to rusty old wood. I am in a house, but how? I look around, I can only see a window. I approach it. The window turns into a door. I step outside. It looks like sand for miles. I walk for miles. Just going straight. I look down, I see a hand appear. It points to the sky...

Liam Michael Taylor (14)
Aldworth School, Basingstoke

Gatland

As I walked down the street I could see an old man asking for money as everyone walked past. I stopped and walked over to him and gave him some money and as I walked away he came back and attacked me, taking my purse. I tried to call the police, but then remembered there are no rules in this land. I was scared and shocked so decided to go and hide in a shelter with my mum and dad. At least then I finally knew that I would be safe from trouble and wouldn't get attacked once again.

Jamie Chatterton (15)
Aldworth School, Basingstoke

Minutes

In 2017, on Earth, there were 250 births a minute. By 2050, Earth was empty; the last person had died, lonely, the only survivor of WW3. But he wasn't alone. Beneath the surface, scientists had developed a way to make people live life in one precious minute. Trillions lived there, under their watchful eyes, in a colossal room filled with young and old people that exist, love, age and die, all in a minute. Humans were bred for the perfect new generation.

The scientists succeeded. In 2053, I was the first person on Earth, mutated to never grow old... alone.

Lariana Sandulescu (13)

Calthorpe Park School, Fleet

A Nazi Ending

'Get down!' shouted the last British captain. The Nazi order fired one last bomb. This killed the captain and many others. The British soldiers then stumbled blindly into battle, getting wiped out by the remaining Nazi soldiers. The Nazis had won not only the battle but the war as well, and the few remaining soldiers saluted Hitler and the Nazi order, as they now knew that they were in power, of the whole world. They were the leaders, and anyone that dared approach them would either bow down, or die. It was certain now that the Nazis ruled the world.

Nathan Wilson (14)
Cantell Maths & Computing College, Bassett

Imagination

I decided. I will die soon so it doesn't matter if something goes wrong. I swallowed the pill and closed my eyes. After a few seconds, a picture appeared in my mind. A beautiful, natural forest materialised and my eyes became flooded with tears. Because of my disease, I couldn't leave hospital. Thanks to an amazing scientist, I can create a place where I can be happy. In the forest the trees were dancing and birds were singing delightful songs. In last days of my life I finally smiled. Suddenly, I felt weak.... I closed my eyes... light...

Wiktoria Krypa (14)
Cantell Maths & Computing College, Bassett

Darkness

It was one in the morning; the rain pattered dismally against the tinted panes and the candles were flagging the dented walls. By the glimmer of the half extinguished light I saw its eyes peeping.

Seconds later, the wind hustled around, breezing through the corners of my eyes. Darkness enveloped me. Following my shadow, I fell flat. The sound echoed and creaked around the room as I heaved my legs against the desk. I took a moment trying to settle myself down, but I felt it. It had me by its palm and I fell straight down, breathless...

Yousham Seenauth (14)
Cantell Maths & Computing College, Bassett

Danger In The Subway

One day a team of friends received a message that there was an explosive device hidden in New York. Someone from Australia was threatening to detonate it. The team of friends had to do something! Everybody got to work on their laptops to figure out how to hack into the explosive's computer system. 'I've done it!' cried Jake. Everyone rushed over.

'Yes!' shouted Bob.

'Now to find this device and destroy it!' said Michael.

They travelled to New York and began hunting.

'It's in the subway, let's go.'

They found it and using careful calculation, carried out a controlled explosion.

Jamie Hegarty (12)

Crestwood College, Eastleigh

The Great Escape

Running, still running, getting nowhere. Emily stumbled past alleyways and into the darkness. Suddenly, hands cupped over her mouth. She tried to scream, no noise. She went black.

Hours had passed when she awoke again. *Where am I?* she thought.

'Hello little girl,' the voice stalked her. A tall dark figure jumped out, revealing his identity. He was dressed with a black cloak with a darkness surrounding his face. Looking around she saw a shiny box with stains over all walls. The dark figure walked closer and closer. He started to pull down his hood when, *bang!* 'What!'

She ran.

Amy Ricketts (12)
Crestwood College, Eastleigh

Destruction Occurred!

Bang! Another historic building collapses, making cars beep. 'What happened to this pretty place?' Lonely as a lamb, Tom swallowed his guilt and searched everywhere. As he stumbled stiffly through the event, he felt he swallowed more guilt and felt more stiff. 'Why did I ever turn against you?' he whispered. 'Am I the only one alive?' As he began to look around the hideous sight, he remembered the haunting event. 'Ready, set, shoot!' bellowed Tom. 'I don't want to keep a single mechanical toy!' As Tom roared at the robots, they marched rigidly towards his daughter and then... *Bang!*

Zakia Bashir (15)
Crestwood College, Eastleigh

Never-Ending Mind Games

'Help!' The only thing I could ever say. I wasn't happy, I wasn't living. Everything was just a continuous nightmare, even if it's just in my mind. I'm surrounded by people talking nonsense, crying and screeching, being extremely loud. 'So stop!' you might say. 'Just make it stop!'

I can't. I can't stop it when it's not real. But you wouldn't understand, you're not like me, no one is. I'm walking by myself. I wish someone could hear me scream out for help, but they can't. I'm in my own messed-up world. I can't escape this hell I created.

Mimi Bartlett (14)
Crestwood College, Eastleigh

Faraway Land

My whole body shakes; jolting up from a sleeping position. Looking around, all I see is pure oak wood. A door, camouflaging against the 'tree' building. Stammering towards the handle, I throw the door open, greeted by tall mushrooms creating a canopy over my head. Holes everywhere I look. 'Where am I?' I whisper, my jaw dropping.

'Welcome to Faraway Land, Ruth! I'm Mr Hatter. The best rabbit in the land!'

Falling, I gasp, 'You know me?'

'Come with me,' the odd, talking Hatter said. My eyes followed the path of the rabbit. Curiously, I decided to follow his footsteps.

Emma Cox (13)
Crestwood College, Eastleigh

Mars Disaster

Frank and Albert stepped out from the shuttle, they had successfully reached Mars! They started traversing Mars when they came across a new life form, never seen before. They quickly rushed back to the ship, only to find out that the 'aliens' were harmless. Daringly, Albert then decided to head over to greet this species, but to his surprise, he had deceived himself and the only reason the 'aliens' didn't attack at first was because they never entered their sight. Then the aliens ended Albert gruesomely with giant rockets and bombarded their ship. Now Frank was desperately fighting for survival.

Jude Fry (12)
Crestwood College, Eastleigh

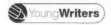

Diego Garcia

Trey, 17, lived in Toronto, Canada, with his mum, dad and brother.

'Next!' shouted the guard.

Peyton, 15 years of age, lived in Chicago with her mum and sister.

'Next!' shouted the guard.

'Welcome to Diego Garcia!' exclaimed the chief. 'You lucky ones are survivors from the apocalypse and destruction of this world.'

They inject and experiment on me daily, then I go back to my cell and just stare at a blank wall, watching the memories of me and my brother flash before me. Why am I here? What are they really after? It's time I found the answers.

Naomie Ang Ting Hone (15)
Crestwood College, Eastleigh

Untitled

Everything was perfect. I walked through the small village, taking notice of my surroundings. Small houses were around, gardens beautifully decorated with flowers and plants. I saw people around, getting their jobs done. Shopping, gardening, cleaning. However, a pained look showed on all of their faces. Usually, everyone was happy, a smile covering their face. Suddenly, everything started disappearing. Houses. Shops. Farms. Everything was gone. I was alone. I was alone and extremely afraid. What was happening? Was this a dream? Soon enough, everything was gone. Alone... for the first time in my life.

Rosie Farmer (13)
Crestwood College, Eastleigh

Anubis Ambush

There was once a woman called Ana Yaromadi. She had a smart daughter called Pharah. One beautiful day they got a warning about a Talon raid. Ana and Pharah ran outside and an airship landed. Villainous Doomfist stepped out of the Talon airship. Ana and Pharah ran towards the temple. Doomfist chased them. He knew about Pharah's pretention as a military rocket jumper. A Brazilian skater shot Doomfist with a sound gun. Doomfist was stunned. Ana and Pharah used this opportunity to sprint away. They got to the temple and Doomfist was already there with Lucio dead on his shoulder...

Ethan Doherty (13)
Crestwood College, Eastleigh

Underground

The underground and its secrets were hidden for centuries until today. Matt ventured down the ancient steps, narrowly avoiding booby traps. It wasn't until he reached flat ground that the true beauty was revealed. Shielding his eyes, Matt reached for the brightest rock. As he grabbed the rock and his face lit up, arrows were released from every angle. Arrows pierced Matt's shoulder, causing him to scream in agony! He turned and ran. He forgot about the traps! Flaming arrows targeted him. Fighting for his life, he never stopped. But he didn't reach it. The diamond rolled back down slowly.

Jack Kemp (15)
Crestwood College, Eastleigh

Alone

Alone. In a place like no other. Brainwashed humans stumble around like zombies. Repetitive routine, day in and out, every day the same, my life's a misery. It hasn't always been like this though, things used to be different but now I spend every day of my life trying to escape. Running breathlessly around streets, trying to find an escape route. Two men stumble behind me, trying to catch up. Although I'm in pain, my chest tightens, my head spins, I keep going. I'll find a better world. Somehow I'm hoping the day will come soon so I'm not alone.

Kira Thorn (15)
Crestwood College, Eastleigh

Avalanche

Looking out at the village, bustling people smile and wave as they go about their daily lives. 'Enni, come quick!' Father yells from the quarry.

Peering down, my head spins as I squint at the faraway chalk at the bottom. 'Hey, pass me the pickaxe.'

Reaching for the weapon, I scream in fear, the rocks are falling. 'Father, Father, get out!' Crashing and thumping as they plummet to the ground, the shrieking stops as the life is washed away. Sobbing inconsolably, I run back to our house and collapse on my bed - he's gone now, it's just me - alone.

Lauren Wood (12)
Crestwood College, Eastleigh

Pixels

Tears trickled down her face like a waterfall. Her body fell lifelessly onto her duvet. Her mother was gone forever. As she attempted to stand up a small piece of paper fell to the floor. She picked it up and studied it: 'Computer, click, pixels!' It was from her mum. She hurried over to her computer and noticed a file called 'Pixels'. What happened next was unexplainable. Her body was sucked into the computer. When she opened her eyes she saw beautiful mountains, lakes and a city in the centre. Colour filled her eyes. Was she dreaming? Welcome to Pixels.

Charlotte Quinn (13)
Crestwood College, Eastleigh

The Last Trees

As I wander away from the battle I spot the lush green trees of Steel Cliffs and I wonder, *will I see these again in my lifetime?* The war between the supremes, brutes and humans rages on behind me, and it sounded like dozens of earthquakes happening at once, or like a few volcanic eruptions. Suddenly the ugly humanoid dogs, named stragglers, rise up from the ground, baring their teeth like snarling wolves about to attack. I take my moonstone blade out of the sheath and begin to hack, slash. Their necks and chests split open, their blood flows freely.

Sam Coker (12)
Crestwood College, Eastleigh

The Mysterious Creation

The world was silent. No movement was heard from all around. Jon was sprinting around the courtyard, stumbling over twigs. Suddenly, a beam of light bounced down from the sky. Jon was curious and went to look. An object so small was there, lifeless, on the ground. The object was small and spherical. Jon was unable to keep it in his hands because of excitement. Jon then thought about life. A human popped up ten metres away from him. He then thought of buildings. There was then bricks in front of him. Could this be the creation that heals humanity?

Katy Jayne Laidler (13)

Crestwood College, Eastleigh

The Unicorn

Lily was twelve. She was very unhappy and disappointed that she had argued with her so-called friends. She sat by a deep purple pool. There were reflections of rainbows in the ripples. Lily began to cry. When she opened her eyes she saw a shimmering unicorn reflected in the pool in front of her. She quickly turned around and there it was. The unicorn had a multicoloured rainbow tail and a golden horn with pink sparkling glitter. Rapidly, the unicorn jumped over her head and splashed into the pool. Lily followed the unicorn into the pool to Unicorn Land.

Hollie Keeling (12)
Crestwood College, Eastleigh

Untitled

Another normal day on Earth. All the humans and dinosaurs were doing fine. The humans were trading items as usual. I went for a walk outside my base then I discovered some dodos so I tamed them and returned them to my base. Then I heard my dinosaurs squealing and grunting, it was a huge carnivore destroying my base and eating all my dinos. The humans, such as me, are supposed to be friendly with the dinosaurs and they're friendly back. But this wasn't working as the T-rex was repeatedly taking bites on my base. Everything was dead and gone!

Oliver Doughty (13)
Crestwood College, Eastleigh

The Attack Of The Ghouls

I slammed my body into the front door repeatedly until it swung open. The smell of mould filled the room, distracting me from escaping. Sprinting upstairs onto the landing area, all doors were sealed shut. I unholstered my AR-15 and put a new magazine in. I started shooting and ghouls were falling everywhere. Just as I thought of reloading, a ghoul caught onto my arm. Its jaw was locked and I did the same anyone would. I pulled the pin on my only grenade, threw it and stabbed deep into my forearm. That cut off all circulation and saved me.

Jack Cox (15)
Crestwood College, Eastleigh

District 7

The shrill alarm bell rings throughout the district for the 8 o'clock pick-up for fruit and veg. Dad and Oliver are in the kitchen eating breakfast. Dad's leaving to work on the farm, he's always there. Shortly after, Oliver leaves on his bike to package the fruit and veg for the next pick-up. Every day around 9 o'clock I walk to the edge of the district and look over the barbed wire fence, imagining what it would be like as one of those people on the other side. The women on the other side look a lot nicer than here.

Rosie Pearce (14)

Crestwood College, Eastleigh

The Beginning Of The End

I woke in a pile of rubble, devoured by the darkness. I felt dreary but I pulled myself together and started to lift the rocks. Surprisingly, they were easy to lift and as the light seeped in, I realised that my hands were purple! I climbed out of the ravine and I realised that I was developing abilities! I saw a corrupted world... People were addicted to little blocks with light coming out of them. I began to gain altitude and I realised that I was not mortal anymore! 'Listen to me,' I said as the people turned and looked.

Rohan Mohindra (13)
Crestwood College, Eastleigh

Zland

Safe haven was only a rumour, nobody knew if it was true. However we were ready to take a leap, if it was the only way away from this dreadful place. With food being scarce and numbers shortened, we stepped foot outside. The atmosphere was thin and the scorching sun blinded us as we crept past the hordes of bloodthirsty zombies. We walked for miles to reach the barrier of the safe haven. All without thought we rushed up the side of the crumbled building, only to witness no trace of safety, only death lay upon our trembling eyes.

Josh Obeney (13)
Crestwood College, Eastleigh

Psycho Sara And The Four Campers

The boot clunked shut. The four passengers got in the car and set off to protest against the empire. Just two hours into their trip the engine blew up. As Jack and Lloyd poked around with the engine, Lloyd felt a sick blow to the back of the head. Jack locked himself inside the car as the psychopath loomed over the bonnet after decapitating Lloyd. She turned and made a horrible grin with her black teeth. She then said, 'You can't stay in that car forever and when you leave I will kill you,' then she laughed evilly.

Logan Thomas Bottomley

Crestwood College, Eastleigh

Police Overdrive

This morning I was scared about what was going to happen, but now that I have escaped it doesn't really bother me.
It all started when I woke up today. I looked out the window and I could see it happening; the thing everyone in this town was dreading. It was the day the robot police tried to take over this world! They said they wanted to make the town better than this dark, destroyed world but no one believes them, apart from me. So I'm going to help them and we will make everything better for the people together.

Emily Muncey (15)
Crestwood College, Eastleigh

Trapped

We had to get out, even with a mind reader, invisible people that walk through solid objects and me a shape-shifter, it was impossible. I told everyone to think of a plan. There was an air vent on the ceiling, no one could possibly reach it. Suddenly, Lucy had an idea; some could stand on others' shoulders and I could get through the vent as a cat. I got out and unlocked the door with no one spotting me. I opened the door, everyone came out. We got outside the building and it was all dead. There was no one.

Eleanor McGeachy (13)
Crestwood College, Eastleigh

Welcome To The Lonely Planet

I woke up, nobody to be seen, alone and no one to talk to. I was extremely confused with what must be going on. All that was around me was shattered stones and torn up gravel everywhere. I sat up and a broken branch glided against my head, I wiped dust off my clothes. I was scared. What had happened to me, because the last thing I even remember was being knocked out and waking up in a cold, lonely background. It was so destroyed, like someone has just wrecked everything and demolished the place and left me to rot.

Morgan Barrass (15)
Crestwood College, Eastleigh

Untitled

In a galaxy far, far away at war the droids invaded the gungans' home so the gungans fought back against the droids, but the droids were too powerful because they had laser tanks which would destroy their home in a blink of an eye, but the gungans lived in water. They had a secret base underwater so it would be very hard for the droids to attack them when they were underwater because only the flower droids can go underwater. So in the end the droids freed the post and the gungan home was left in bogs.

Ben Edwards (13)
Crestwood College, Eastleigh

Monster Ville!

Fright hits me with a flash! I stare at the face-like building with my little sister in the corner. I walk outside and gasp for air as smoke flutters out of the top of the chimney. Distant screams of my little sister lure me closer and closer. Oh no! Where is she? Where has she gone? I search and search down the street top to bottom. There is only one house I didn't check! The haunted house. What will I do now? Oh my god, the street is silent, very silent, no one around. Silence, danger and horror!

Maya Ray (12)
Crestwood College, Eastleigh

Untitled

Ever had the feeling that something bad was going to happen? That's how I had felt. I woke up in the middle of the night dazed. Nothing was as I remembered it. I felt paralysed. I didn't know why. I tried to go back to sleep as if it was a dream but I felt unusually energetic. A figure appeared randomly. A man? It looked like he had some kind of syringe in his hand. He pulled a sharp object from his pocket and pointed it at my stomach. He whispered, 'Boo!' and then, *slash!*

Jamie Clegg (13)
Crestwood College, Eastleigh

Untitled

Bang! The bullet went through an alien's head with green blood squirting out everywhere. I finally realised that I was in my room but I was shrunk down, no wonder everything looked big. I looked up and saw a monster on a throne or something because he was staring at me. Then he sent lots of his troops so it was time to strike so I had to go and fight. Suddenly, I could hear loud footsteps. The door cracked open... It was my mum, she said it was the end of playtime.

Tyler Darley (11)
Crestwood College, Eastleigh

Escape

The door refused to move, I could hear the ghosts tumbling down the corridor. They wouldn't be pleased. Their mind control had finally began to break, letting me have my own thoughts, but also meaning their forms were beginning to go. I couldn't see them as well as before. I felt the air chill as the ghosts' presence was getting closer than ever. The door still wouldn't move. The lock stood its ground. I crouched down, concentrating on picking this tight jammed lock. *Click!* The lock slid open, sending light streaming from the cracks. I'd made it, just in time.

Ruthie Quinn (12)
Oaklands Catholic School & Sixth Form College, Waterlooville

Trapped Kingdom

I'm lost. It's cramped and there's a dull light above me. I'm in an endless passageway with pipes creeping up the walls and heavy cogs lying against the tin structure surrounding me. Venturing on through a wondrous world of mechanics, I see ladders as tall as skyscrapers. There are iron doors locked and unopened. As I carry on through the dim light the corridor widen until I reach a window. From the glass I see a war zone of rubble and ruins, but I can't see any life. Then I realise I'm lost inside the walls, inside a trapped kingdom.

Bethany Kate Saunders (12)

Oaklands Catholic School & Sixth Form College, Waterlooville

Death's Journey

Falling. That's how it all started. All I can remember is a cream-white unicorn named Andy, a red dragon called Fury and him, the dwarf who made me be murdered. The dwarf who told Amanda the psycho ghost, who was after me. Who murdered me! After discovering Malaga I was told to leave. I didn't listen. Without letting myself leave I let Malaga be destroyed as well as the two innocent friends of mine who lived in Malaga. Unfortunately, Amanda discovered me in this hidden wonderland and set out to murder me. Dead. That's what I am now. Completely dead.

Katherine Esther Gamboa-Kerwood (12)
Oaklands Catholic School & Sixth Form College, Waterlooville

Rescued

It has been seventy-eight days since the illness started, and sixty-four days since we were 'rescued'. They came and took us away from our families, not allowed to take a single item with us, not even the cat. They took us to a building, a tall, white, prison-like building. They pushed us into a room filled with about twenty other children. The opaque door slammed behind us, and a deep, menacing voice spoke out, saying how lucky we were and that this was our home now. I escaped. I am dying. I caught the illness. I guess we were rescued.

Emily Poppy Lipman (13)
Oaklands Catholic School & Sixth Form College, Waterlooville

The Beach

As John stood on the beach he used to love, he saw an ocean of misery glaring at him. This was the place his father had died nine months ago.

Since then he had never been back, however today something had drawn him here. A sense of mystery hung in the air. Suddenly from far away, a huge wave sprang up from nowhere. Heavy rain poured from the heavens. As Josh sprinted up the beach, he heard his father's voice saying, 'Stay, the wave will swallow you and you will enter my kingdom.' Josh left his home, he was gone...

Athene Ryan (12)

Oaklands Catholic School & Sixth Form College, Waterlooville

The Rise Of A Nature Hero

The mighty Oak, God of Nature created all this. Tree men for knights and they found slaves. There is no peace. No one is equal. They need a hero but who can it be?
One small sapling was sitting watching. He needed to do something. He charged at the mighty Oak and threw a spear through the branch of him and he fell to the ground, dead! Everything was back to normal and there was no evil god. Waiting the sapling was, for the recreation of Treezem. One god stood there, good god and he was there creating his world, Earth.

Beau Rimmer (12)

Oaklands Catholic School & Sixth Form College, Waterlooville

What War Does

'Come on Caitlin! We don't have long to get our rations.'
'Alright, I'm coming! Remember you promised we'd go to the park, OK?'
We walked down the illuminated red lit-up road towards the park. We hated the war. It always brought bad news. 'Can you push me on the swings now Charlie?'
I was really tired and wanted to go. 'No, we need to go.' We walked home chatting and laughing.
'Mum, we're home!'
We walked into the living room to find Mum crying. Her lips trembled. 'Girls... ' We waited. 'Dad's dead.' My sister collapsed. Now the war's started.

Charlie Knight (13)
The Clere School, Burghclere

Is It Really You?

I saw her standing at the platform for the next hovercraft to London. I rubbed my eyes, it couldn't really be. My sister couldn't be alive, she had been dead for a year. 'Hannah,' I shouted, 'is that you?'

The blonde figure turned and ran towards me. 'Joe!' Hannah exclaimed. 'Ooh, how I've missed you!'

'Hannah, how are you not dead, why are you hovering to London?' I questioned.

'I must go, I'll miss my hovercraft.'

'Stay and tell me why you are doing this,' I begged.

'No, it's not safe, I must go, before they find you too Joe!'

Mollie Johnson (12)
The Clere School, Burghclere

Capital Of Cards

'Osaka Najimo, what are you doing?' shouted Yuki Nogami. 'Fighting for my country!' he shouted as his fists pummelled the wall to the basement of the cabinet building. Dust flew everywhere as the wall crashed and they set the timers on the explosives. Once a safe distance away, the rebels formed to watch the fireworks of the cabinet building, and its inhabitants exploding. Uproar sprouted around the band of merry men as they watched the no-good capital crumble before them. This was usual to them and therefore no one batted even a single eyelid. No one noticed them leave.

Lewis Samuel Williams (11)

The Clere School, Burghclere

Wings

Huffing, the demon shoved the blue-haired enemy across the room. Isogai spat insults at him. 'Urgh! You really disgust me.' He stepped up to Riku, pressing him to the old, hard floor with his hand firmly gripping the angel's thin neck. A strong punch to Riku's stomach caused his body to fall limp, exhausted. His wings twitched uselessly and he hung his head. Once again Riku had been undoubtedly defeated by the black-eyed demon. How shameful. Isogai smirked, letting Riku's body fall to the floor like a lifeless marionette. 'You always have been weak.' With that, he strode away.

Ellie-Anne Stoodley (13)

The Clere School, Burghclere

Forever Forgotten

On a planet far, far away lies Candyland and their people are jelly. They've heard that they're going to be attacked by the humans down on Earth.

The next day, the Jellies start to prepare for the attack. The humans jump in their rocket and fly to Candyland. Once they arrive at Candyland they dive right into everything because it's made out of candy. At this point the Jellies are slowly melting. The humans, on the other hand, think they're at home, scoffing their faces.

About a week later, Candyland has disappeared and all the Jellies have melted.

Jamie Harrison (12)
The Clere School, Burghclere

White Ash

Ruby sat on the newly found beach, looking at the evening sunset whilst it created a soft, golden glow against the calm water. *What would've happened if I didn't find the exit?* she thought. *Why is Osterra, the world of constant war, so empty?* She dipped her toes into into the salty cold water, trying to think of an answer to them. Ruby sighed, stroking her fingers over her teacher Errol's jade dragon pin. It was too late however, as another question was about to cross her mind. Why was her teacher covered in blood, standing right behind her?

Cody Logan Marsh (13)
The Clere School, Burghclere

Man's Death Future

As the door opened, two brave soldiers glimpsed at the destroyed world with burning and collapsing buildings, disappearing people and police patrolling and guarding the president. Deep inside, both of them knew they had to rescue the president before it was too late. If they failed they knew it would change history forever. One of the soldiers checked the six-hour countdown until the president died there was only four hours left and they knew he was at the top floor of the Empire State Building. 'Just remember, we cannot disappear until we have the president, we must be careful!'

Jonny Powis (12)
The Clere School, Burghclere

Father Time

He woke up. Today was the day. The day he would finally see his parents again. He glanced over at the mysterious 'portal' looking thing. His legs stumbled as he carried them over to the alien structure. He stood there, thoughts racing through his head... *Should I jump?*
What will happen if I do? He stood there, still frozen in thought, staring blankly. He had made a decision, took a deep breath and jumped... *Thump!* He landed onto a cold concrete floor. The boy picked himself up and trembled over to a door, opened it and entered the outside world.

Jack Kitson (11)
The Clere School, Burghclere

The Dog Heist

Abi and Bella, scientists, were working on an experiment to double the size of dogs. 'Bella, to do this we need a dog!' Abi stuttered.

The scientists decided the only way to get a dog was to steal one! They decided to go to a dog-walking field...

'There it is! The perfect dog! Go on Bella, you go grab it,' Abi grimaced.

'I-I can't do this... ' Bella sprinted off into the distance, hoping Abi would commit the crime. Abi shuffled home in anger, until she spotted a dog the size of a house and Bella standing next to it guiltily.

Libby Machin (13)
The Clere School, Burghclere

Mutation

As Hazel and Tony walked out of the front doors of a destroyed school that was their camp, they saw on the scorching hot, barren landscape, a pack of mutant creatures shredding another mutant creature into pieces. 'Filthy things they are... ' said Tony as his throat seized up with anger and sadness.

Hazel put a hand on his shoulder. Tony's parents were killed by those disgusting things. They stood there for a moment as they watched all the pus run across the dirt. In the gloom behind a figure stood, blood dripping from his ugly scarred face... They turned around...

Angus Mills (13)
The Clere School, Burghclere

Possessed

I heard the baby crying and shouting, 'Dzuma, Dzuma!' I don't know what that means. I don't speak Polish. 'Dzuma!' shouted the baby. I had a feeling that it was possessed by some kind of demon. 'Dzuma!' shouted the baby. Blood poured out of her mouth, her eyes slowly turned pitch-black. I called the church. 'Dzuma!' shouted the baby. I tried to put her to sleep and I gave her milk but she spat it back out. Then I heard knocking on the door. I went to see who it was. It was the priest, he said, 'Dzuma!'

Miki Jarzembowski (12)
The Clere School, Burghclere

They Want Me

Footsteps. Closer and closer. The door was open. Running. I was running faster than ever. They were after me - I just knew it. Desperate to find my parents. My heart pounding like a drum, sweat dribbling and knees trembling I searched. Then right there; down below me - I saw them. A single tear rolled down my face. My mum, my dad; the people there to protect me - gone. Gone forever. Their nemesis had killed them. What happens from here? I'm just a teenage girl. *Rustle.* The leaves twitched. They were here - here for me. 'Aaaah! Where are you taking me?'

Amandi Mendis (12)
The Clere School, Burghclere

Falling London

I saw it on the news this evening. Families still mourning, grieving quietly. Soon it will become louder and reverberate around the world and shake like an earthquake. The plane hit Buckingham Palace at 5:27pm. Mum headed to London looking for a job this morning. Still sobbing, trying to find her contact on my phone. She didn't pick up, again I tried, no sound. It's only a mile away from my house to Buckingham Palace and the place Mum tried to get a place with this job. Had she been affected?
I ran fast and saw her lying, bleeding.
'Help!'

Genevieve Jacklin (12)
The Clere School, Burghclere

What If?

Bang, bang! Gunshots pierced my ears with their blood-curdling screams. 1939-1945; six years without my family and still the war isn't over. 'Why, w-why!'

Orders from my general came in. 'Whatever the cost, shoot the person in charge!'

Every able man then charged to any place to aim and try and kill the person in charge. Then, out of the corner of my eye, I spotted him. Now was the time! I now knew what to do. I knelt down, aimed my gun while breathing hard, then pulled the trigger! He was dead... Hitler was dead...

Tyler Sean Alison (12)
The Clere School, Burghclere

Trapped!

As I glanced around me, I saw the same old scenery closing in on me. Another repetitive day lay ahead of me, trapped in this soul-destroying, caged nightmare. Already, the first visitors were arriving and the peace I craved was shattered by piercing sounds of screeching children banging the glass. Turning my back on them, I preened my glossy striped fur. Anger raged inside me. Why did I have to suffer this unbearable life? The noise echoed through my head; I couldn't take it anymore. I pounced at the glass window, wishing these torturous humans could be my lunch.

Amy Hopgood (11)
The Clere School, Burghclere

Daredevil Josh

Once, there was a boy called Josh, he was a daredevil with his right-hand man, George. Their plan was to rob the Crown Jewels with a Lamborghini as their getaway vehicle. As they slowly approached the Tower of London, George got shaky. They entered the tower, all they had to do was kill the guards which wouldn't be easy. As they were looking, George put the laser glasses on. As he was about to strike, a voice said, 'Oi, what are you doing?'
Josh and George ran away, however nobody knows, will they strike back ever again?

Danny Pither (12)
The Clere School, Burghclere

The Letter

A letter dropped through the letter box last Sunday, hidden between a brochure for a new boiler and a postcard from France, meant for him next door. I recognised the handwriting immediately. I haven't opened it yet. It's been sitting on the mantelpiece leaning against that old clock you gave me. I can't work out why you've written to me after all these years. I'm also wondering as to how you did it considering I killed you five years ago and buried you under the patio. Maybe I will open it tomorrow, just to see what you want. Again.

Kenzii Aitken-Thompson (11)
The Clere School, Burghclere

Alone In The Unknown

Awake. Alone. Confused. I lay in silence, trying to focus my dizzy mind. No light. No smells. No tastes. Nothing. Then a bright, somewhat familiar light swallowed me as I watched myself sink into the icy water. Helpless, I was thrown back vigorously into the dark reality, once again alone and confused. My ears rang as I heard muffled voices above. I gave a cry which, to my surprise, was silent. I tried to move but was greeted with no movement. Darkness hit me once again as I fell back into the void. The voices faded. Alone. Confused. Dizzy. Asleep.

Lauren Ann Osborne (13)

The Clere School, Burghclere

Dark Earth

It was dark. He felt warm breath on his neck. Turning around, he found no one there. Shivering, he felt around for an escape. He found a handle and pulled it sharply. Stepping out into the burning sun, he squinted as he saw the peril that the world was in. He staggered backwards in horror. What happened... ? He shook his head sharply; continuing for miles he watched the despair of survivors looking for loved ones. He picked up a stone and watched it file through his fingers like dust. What had he done? He came to a conclusion. He did this.

Cerys Deakin (12)
The Clere School, Burghclere

Atomic Trust

As I look over the horizon, I hear a scream. I swerve around to see no one. 'I should go inside before the radiation gets to me if there is anymore radiation,' I say. Slowly I make my way back to the bunker. 'You're crazy! You cannot be trusted,' I hear. Sighing, I carry on. By now having someone shout is normal, especially trusting others. Even if it's been 200 years since the nuclear explosion, people will not trust others, I don't trust them, the people or the so-called government. They are all out to get me.

Hannah Gaff (12)

The Clere School, Burghclere

Reaction

I come to the cave. Blue blaring lights shine down! I see them. The raiders who cracked me over the head, back at the camp. I soon realise that I am being dragged towards a tank filled with a strange green liquid. It has a motor cable on the cylinder. Callius hydroxide (neuro-toxin). I immediately understand how they were killing off us redwoods by drowning us in neuro-toxins. A janitor stands by a corpse pile. I kick and struggle until I escape the grasp of the raiders and I run. I run fast to the entrance. Again darkness.

Cameron Vincent (13)
The Clere School, Burghclere

You Always Learn More...

Washing my arm with soap, I then closed my eyes and entered. Turning to my apprentice, George (whose breath was on fire from a chilli he ate earlier) I commented, 'You always know more by shoving your hand up a creature's bum!' As George took a deep breath, I could feel my arm getting hotter and hotter the more it lost circulation. In all my years as a vet I had never had such an uncomfortable examination. I pulled my hand out - which had started to go blue. The mother roared in huge pain... and out came a baby dragon.

Libby Jonas (11)
The Clere School, Burghclere

110

The Ferret's Claw

The lights flash as we scuttle across the grassy floor. Fur coats start speeding round my teammate. He falls down, claw marks all over his body. Bushes rustling, as three ferrets charge out towards my furry neck. I slash back, cutting their legs. They collapse as I run around to avenge my friend. There are four ferrets left; myself and the deadly duo. The death cannon sounds for every fallen foe. Suddenly silence as the duo charge from different directions, claws out. I jump out just in time as they fall. The Ferret Games are over.

Jonathan David Spence (13)
The Clere School, Burghclere

Just Once

Stepping up a mountain, I finally reach a narrow cave so dark I can't even see past the opening. I suddenly realise how grubby and wet the outside appearance is. I am in. There is no one here except a few rocks and stones. Hold on a minute, what was that, something just tickled my back. Help! I can hear water heading my way. It is getting louder and louder and louder. It's got me, it's pushing me. It's stopped and somehow I've landed on a fluffy cloud. Wait, I have just been up Libby's nose. Oh no. Oh gosh.

Darcy Drummond (12)
The Clere School, Burghclere

The Winning 'One'

I stepped up to the stand, my gun in hand and 500 eyes on me. Thoughts were spinning around my head like a roller coaster. I saw the small round disc coming towards me. I quickly pulled my gun up, focused my eyes, aimed 1... 2... 3... *Bang!* The bullet shot out, making the gun smash into my shoulder. It was over, I didn't want to look to see if I got it. Suddenly it went from silence to cheering. I turned to my dad to see a tear rolling down his face.
'Did I get it?'
'Yes Lily, yes!'

Lily Soper (13)
The Clere School, Burghclere

Eso The Dragonborn

Eso was on his way to Whiterun when a sudden roar echoed through the sky. A dragon swooped down to grab him, but luckily it just missed.

He ran, but halted as he came towards a merchant house. Eso had sworn to Talos and all there that he would protect them. So he pulled out his ebony bow and began shooting arrows. It was a long but great battle, Eso shot his last arrow and it pierced the dragon's wing, it fell to the ground with a mighty thud. He approached the beast and stole its scales for armour.

Cameron Digance (13)

The Clere School, Burghclere

Time Bomb

I'm running fast. My sister, Chloe, is just ahead of me. The tunnel which led to safety was just around this corner. Bodies of our brave soldiers lay on the roads. Piles of rubble where there had once been houses. Suddenly, Chloe shouted for help. She'd fallen over. I could see the army plane edging towards us. I ran over to her, helping her up. She then reached safety. I tried to run too but my skirt was caught on a twig. I tugged at it but it was too late. The planes were above me. Bombs fell out. *Bang!*

Thurka Ananth (12)
The Clere School, Burghclere

Army

I really miss my family, my wife is at home with the kids drawing pictures on the kitchen table. My mate's getting ready for training. I loved the army once but that was two years ago, I have put my notice in already, just have to wait one more year. 'Please General, I really want to go now.' I would beg but it would never work.

'Too many excuses, you think we can let you go and keep everyone else,' he kept telling me, so I went to the general's boss and he let me go. I ran home, overjoyed.

Phoebe Maxwell-Heron (12)
The Clere School, Burghclere

Here Lies The Key To Happiness

It had been five years since the galactic war, but Cory was still uncomfortable, even if he was happy under the two suns of Seronia. He thought about his situation as he entered the temple. When he did, his dog Uni leapt out of his bag. He held out his light as it reflected off the crystals guiding him to what he was searching for. A couple of secrets crawled up to him but just whacked him. He finally found what he was looking for; the rune of life. Cory knew with this he would unlock his happiness...

William Hunter (12)
The Clere School, Burghclere

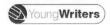

A New Planet

My hand trembled as we were made to get on a spaceship. Worried, as I did not know what was going on, I stepped onto the ship. The doors shut with a bang! We arrived at a place that looked just like Earth, but here there was no war, litter or pollution.

'We put you here because our Earth got ruined so we made this planet into a new one. Look after this planet,' boomed a deep voice.

Slowly we left the ship and the grass was green and real. I could tell I'd like it here very much.

Katie Smith (13)
The Clere School, Burghclere

My Video Game Utopia

I heard a beep as the PlayStation turned on, launching me into the world of my favourite video game. As the hours went by, I became closer to the character's life more than mine. I saw through his eyes as I gazed through the spacecraft's viewing screen, to see a gaping hole in Saturn's rings where there was once planet debris. I pushed my left thumb forward, and instantly the ship hurtled towards Saturn. I knew my mission was to land. I didn't know if I could make it, unsure of what lay ahead.

Nathan Cook (11)
The Clere School, Burghclere

The Welsh Mystery

It all began last week. Me and my friend Jess were diving in Wales when Jess told me she had discovered an old building on a small, quiet island. We slowly swam there whilst looking at the marine wildlife. Suddenly we were swept by a wave and landed safely on the island. Then a boy walked up to us and said, 'Hi, my name is Drake and welcome to the Water World Academy.' He then told us that he had depression and had sadly killed himself before I got to tell him how I felt. My heart was now broken.

Emily Grace Bentham (11)
The Clere School, Burghclere

Survival

I swiftly spin round the corner being careful to not get caught, just thinking about what the Germans might do to me if I'm caught rebelling is making me feel sick. As the sweat on my face drips onto the rock-hard ground I run like there is no tomorrow because there might not be for me at least, in our words this might be my last day on this planet. Sometimes I get the hope that this whole war might, just might, blow over one day, but I don't think that will happen very soon. Goodbye world!

Aaron Cinnamon (11)
The Clere School, Burghclere

The Curse In Egypt

Once, a boy and his parent went to Egypt and he found some big black beetles and found a temple of doom and they were about to buy merchandise but they found out that a missing tablet and the beetles were somehow related so the young boy went to find the missing beetles that they had passed on the way to the temple of doom. Suddenly it collapsed and the only way to stop it from falling was to find that missing tablet. Suddenly there was the tablet shining against the sun. He had to bring it back.

Zachary David Morgan (12)
The Clere School, Burghclere

The Boy Who Built A Den

One day, a boy named Dave, who lived on a farm, was building a den in the woods, which had two storeys with a bed and a chair. As he was just about to finish painting the outside of the den, his dad whistled, and this was Dave's cue to go home for dinner and then go to bed.
The next day he woke up, then he ate breakfast. He then went back to his den and it was gone. Dave stood there and cried. Dave went home to his dad and said, 'It's gone Dad, it's gone Dad!'

Adam Lee Goater (13)
The Clere School, Burghclere

Blown Away

I stood there, looking up to the smoke-filled sky. I could feel the life inside of me slipping away. The gunshots grew quiet and so did the screaming. The dirt that was blown up into the air along with me was now falling onto my face. It was getting in my eyes. I tried moving my arm so I could get it out, but my arm was stuck by my side. I tried sitting up and moving myself but I couldn't. I was helpless. I took a deep breath in, exhaled and then I was gone. Never to return.

Megan Holmes (13)
The Clere School, Burghclere

Why?

I took in a deep breath, the smell of blood and burnt skin filled my throat. I was pushed forward and the sound of chains rang in my ears. I took a step and gasped at the sight before me! Bodies littered the land, like flies to a pile of rubbish. I heard the wails of a child and looked up just in time to see the hand of a beast tear through her. I gasped. Shock racked my body. I visibly shivered as the beast looked me in the face and I asked myself, 'What have I done?'

Millie Leonard (13)
The Clere School, Burghclere

The Woods

My feet tread confidently, despite my heart beating 10 times faster as I contemplate my fate. I hear voices, cold and gnarled. The crunch of crisp snow under my feet grows louder. I hear the sound of screaming, it's so high-pitched I feel as if it's shattering my skull. When I reach the tree I hear, 'Well done Alice, you made it! We wondered when you'd join us.'

My sight begins to spiral as we're sucked into the tree of death and despair...

Madeleine Rose Gant (12)

The Clere School, Burghclere

Missing Part

Why was I doing this? I should have listened to my boyfriend, but no and now I'm about to steal a diamond.
'Cody, I can't do it! What if I get caught?'
'Ella, I need this! It's the final part for my laser gun. Plus you owe me.' He gave me a hug and told me to go.
As I slowly walked towards the diamond, I felt my hands start to sweat beneath my gloves. Why was I doing this? I carefully picked up the diamond...

Caitriona May Langrell (13)
The Clere School, Burghclere

The Missile

I awoke to the sound of gunfire. Steadily, holding onto a pole, I staggered to my feet. The door was two feet away so I pulled it open with all my strength. Suddenly, it flung open. The bright Arabian sun blinded me. A roar of a low-flying jet added more ounces of pain to my already deadly headache. Panicky, I searched for a weapon. Sweat was pouring down my face. But before I could do anything, I heard a shout. 'Missile!' and suddenly it all went black.

Alfie Knox (13)
The Clere School, Burghclere

The Legacy

My name is Mr Bernard, this is to the government: 'I am the leader of a colony of survivors. We survived an outbreak of a rare disease that killed everyone, including my family. I'm dying so I want to leave my people with a gift, a legacy if you will. You see I'm a professor so I'm creating a cure for the disease so my people can reproduce the human race. I am Mr Bernard and this is my legacy'.

Henry Munslow-Barker (14)
The Clere School, Burghclere

The Beginning Of The End

Running, running, twisting round corners, wheezing, trying to catch my breath. Stopping wasn't an option, it would find me. The old, haunted, derelict, mansion's walls closed in on me I quickly turned the rusty knob to my left, my only chance of escaping this horrific nightmare, if only it was a nightmare. But I knew that wouldn't be the case as shockingly unbelievable as this was, it was really happening.

Finally, I entered the long abandoned room. I could sense its presence luring over me and its sickening deathly odour, whatever was hunting me was hunting for my soul.

Josh Logan (14)
The Island Learning Centre, Newport

The Silence Of Panic

The baby cries. Panic filters down the long corridors bringing fear to the Chillingham Care Home. The home was a hot spot for mentally ill patients who were held as prisoners in the 19th century. The building is like a castle but was made into a home after the Mafia War. It has been said there is a patient still burrowing in the hallways. His name is Roberto Winchester also known as the care home creep. The building was built next to a famous monument. There the prison band would bring that tad of happiness to a miserable past.

Shaun Anthony Joseph Moore (15)
The Island Learning Centre, Newport

No Man And The Mixed Earth

'Rocket 194, do you read me? Captain, do you read me?'

'Yes sir,' I breathed frantically.

'Are you OK?'

'Yes I'm... just running out of air. I think I am underwater Sir.'

'You're just-... '

'Sir, Sir!' I shouted. 'OK, I'm all on my own. Perfect,' I said to myself.

'Activating self-destruct sequence,' said COP (co-pilot).

'Three... two... one ... '

'No!' I cried.

'Deactivate self-destruct sequence,' said COP.

'Captain, my air is on critical... I've lost communication.'

As I look out I see a beautiful new world.

'Landing sequence activate,' said COP.

At least I was safe.

Jake Mitchener (12)
The Romsey School, Romsey

Midnight Egg

It's hatching... The world drew silent to see the supernatural event become a reality. An eye opened. Everyone was jumping to see; and that's where it all went wrong... on that fateful day we survivors call 'Shift'.

Three years ago scientists discovered an egg. This had the power to make people invincible so they brought it back to 'Shift-laboratories'. But in trying to obtain the power, it unleashed a mighty terror that took over the world.

The egg released a fog that enveloped the Earth in a black stormy cloud that killed everyone who was outside. Who's invincible now?

Haiden Crook (13)
The Romsey School, Romsey

The Horizon's Ark!

The ship had crash-landed on an unknown planet, Thrae. There were dinosaurs roaming the world and this elite team had been sent to wipe them out.

'Captain, our thrusters are broken, she's going down, hold on.'

'Hello is anyone there? Hello?'

Sergeant James was the only one left, with no guns and no armour against millions of dinosaurs.

'I need a weapon!'

He found some sticks and made a bow, a shack. Now he had to go into a place no one had ever been, all alone with no comrades help him.

'I'm all alone now with the dinosaurs... '

Reece Grimshaw (12)

The Romsey School, Romsey

Untitled

I awoke with a jolt atop my horse, it slowly trailing behind my fellow rider. The sun was high already. Two weeks we had been riding, almost non-stop, and suddenly we were surrounded by beauty. I could almost taste the sweet scent of freshly bloomed roses as I scanned my surroundings. Chirping birds flittered past me in great numbers, singing pleasant tunes as they flew; all while a mild breeze kissed and warmed my travel-dirty face. So much colour, sunlight, movement stretching all the way to the borders.

My awe was suppressed by a few simple words: 'Welcome to Wonderland.'

Rebecca Allison (15)
The Romsey School, Romsey

The Reverse Speedster

It was a furious day in the 21st century; the Speedster won a fight. Suddenly a wormhole opened and out came the Reverse Speedster. He was carrying a big weapon. Bravely, I chased him. After an intense battle he told me his name - John William. He was from the 40th century and without warning he pulled the trigger on the weapon.
I saw a flash of light and then *boom!* I watched in horror as he had just blown up and destroyed half the multiverse. The wormhole opened again so I followed after him...
What's next? I thought.

Cameron Davis (13)
The Romsey School, Romsey

The President Of Earth's Speech

'Venus equals communism. I know that Venus, the city in the clouds, is being run by the Orchid communist party, which has been a great threat to Mars. Mars funds Earth, giving me extreme weapons, for my conquest. So it has come to my realisation that I must use 'Calamity'. Calamity is a mass destruction weapon.

At 11pm Venus time Wednesday, I will be launching Calamity. You will see a colossal beam of purple light, then to be followed by a beautiful fireball in the sky. The losses will be extravagant. It's for the greater good.'

Gareth Lewis-Cole (12)
The Romsey School, Romsey

Paradise's Fighters

Paradise was the new Earth, an amazing place. Big blue oceans, smaller islands, lovely green grass, but with a new Earth comes a new war, this is my story.

June 30th 2042. I was transported to paradise to fight in the war, but when the transport ship landed it was shot by a pulsar cannon. Everyone jutted to one side, I grabbed my Skana and KN-44 then ran out of the ship before it exploded. *Boom!* The ship exploded.

5 hours later... The firing ceased. I had to find a way across no-man's-land to kill Tarus Reiner. Now!

Oliver Pace (13)

The Romsey School, Romsey

My Best Friend's A Dragon

Breathing heavily, I ran for my life. I had bruises on my legs, cuts on my arms, I was in agony. Suddenly, my legs gave way and I fell to what I thought was my end.

Then there she was: a beautiful black-scaled, sharp-winged dragon! However, she seemed different than the other dragons. She wasn't out for blood, she seemed caring and gentle. But what I didn't know was that this magnificent creature was going to help me stop the war between dragons and humans and make peace in the world. She was going to be my friend.

Olivia Taylor (12)
The Romsey School, Romsey

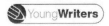

The Life On Bri-An

Keith was walking his dog when he suddenly found himself being eaten by a giant beetle. This was around the point that he fainted.

When he woke up he looked around, saw he was in a jungle and thought, *did I leave the gas on?*

He walked around, finding things beyond the human mind, so they can't be described. When Keith arrived back where he had come to Bri-an (this was the planet's name; I don't know why). He sat down, pondered on life, then decided he would never fit in on Earth. He was home!

Reuben Burbidge (13)

The Romsey School, Romsey

The Falling

1902: The wind was blowing.

We were on a tour round the Romsey Abbey for the first time ever. We eventually got to the top; I was really excited until...

It fell, fell right out my hands. My teddy that my father got me before he passed away.

I couldn't, couldn't just watch it go, so I reached out to grab it, but then the wind came straight at me.

2016: I'm still here, but now no one ever notices me, I've never left this place; never been able to.

I want to go home, but I think I'm trapped.

Jessica Sedman-Lambe (14)
The Romsey School, Romsey

Urge

I close the rusty door to my cheap apartment. I open the fridge. There is a sausage and some macaroni. I put the foul-smelling meat in my mouth. I spit it out; a tear drops on the macaroni. I open the fridge again. I eat anything I see. It all tastes disgusting. *Is it off?* I think to myself. I run outside to get more food, but there's something in the air, something so good my mouth begins to water. I know where the smell is coming from. There's a child at the end of the road...

Chris Blake (13)

The Romsey School, Romsey

Untitled

I was strolling past the woods when I heard *crunch!* A branch had snapped in the woods. I was deciding whether I should see what was happening, so I went in and I followed the sound; *swish, swash,* from the river.

I tripped and fell down a mysterious hole and I hit my head. I was so confused. When I woke up, I slowly stood up and found myself in the future and I saw my parents and my friends...

Jessica Beauchamp (12)
The Romsey School, Romsey

The Eruption!

The scars from the last world were just too much. There I was in my happy world shouting from the top of what was supposed to be a dormant volcano. I was a geothermal scientist on Mars, always exploring new volcanoes but the one time it is meant to be safe was this trip. All the rest were about to blow when I went up there, but not this one.

Jean-Luc Hill-Dobson (13)

The Romsey School, Romsey

YoungWriters
Est.1991

YOUNG WRITERS
INFORMATION

We hope you have enjoyed reading this book – and that you will continue to in the coming years.

If you're a young writer who enjoys reading and creative writing, or the parent of an enthusiastic poet or story writer, do visit our website **www.youngwriters.co.uk**. Here you will find free competitions, workshops and games, as well as recommended reads, a poetry glossary and our blog.

If you would like to order further copies of this book, or any of our other titles, then please give us a call or visit **www.youngwriters.co.uk**.

Young Writers
Remus House
Coltsfoot Drive
Peterborough
PE2 9BF
(01733) 890066
info@youngwriters.co.uk